COGNITIVE-BEHAVIORAL THERAPY IN RELATIONSHIPS:

Techniques and Concepts for Psychotherapists

Michel Lopes

Mix Comunicações

ISBN-13: 9798301411960
ISBN-10: 1477123456

Cover design by: Art Painter
Library of Congress Control Number: 2018675309
Printed in the United States of America

CONTENTS

FOREWORD

In recent years, Cognitive-Behavioral Therapy (CBT) has established itself as one of the most effective and widely used therapeutic approaches for treating various psychological disorders. However, the application of CBT to interpersonal relationships remains an expanding field full of untapped potential. This book, Cognitive-Behavioral Therapy in Relationships: A Complete Guide for Psychotherapists, aims to bridge this gap, offering a comprehensive and practical resource for professionals who wish to enhance their clinical practice skills. Inspired by the style and scientific rigor of the renowned work of Judith S. Beck, this book is carefully crafted to provide a solid theoretical foundation, along with specific techniques and strategies to address the unique challenges of relationships. Whether in the context of couples, families, friendships, or support networks, CBT offers powerful tools to foster mutual understanding, resolve conflicts, and strengthen emotional bonds.

Throughout the chapters, we explore everything from the historical and theoretical foundations of CBT to specific interventions for crisis situations, the use of technology in therapeutic practice, and adaptations for different types of relationships. Detailed case studies and practical examples enrich the content, enabling psychotherapists to visualize the application of techniques in real-world scenarios.

This book is intended for psychotherapists seeking not only to increase their professional competence but also to make a significant difference in the lives of their clients. We invite you to embark on this journey of learning and discovery, confident that Cognitive-Behavioral Therapy has the potential to transform relationships and, consequently, improve people's quality of life.

PREFACE

Cognitive-Behavioral Therapy (CBT) has stood out as an effective and evidence-based therapeutic approach for treating a wide range of psychological disorders. However, its application in the context of interpersonal relationships is an area that deserves special attention, given the complexity and importance of human interactions in our mental health and well-being.

This book, Cognitive-Behavioral Therapy in Relationships: A Complete Guide for Psychotherapists, emerges as a response to this need. Inspired by the pioneering work of Judith S. Beck, this manual aims to provide psychotherapists with a robust and practical tool for intervening in relationships, whether they are romantic, familial, friendly, or professional in nature.

Throughout my career as a psychotherapist and researcher, I have closely observed the challenges people face in their relationships. Issues such as communication, conflict resolution, emotional management, and bond strengthening are recurring themes in clinical practice. CBT offers a theoretical and practical framework capable of addressing these issues effectively and transformatively.

This book is divided into chapters covering everything from the theoretical foundations of CBT to specific intervention techniques, including detailed case studies and practical examples. The goal is to offer a guide that not only educates but also inspires and equips psychotherapists to apply CBT effectively in their clinical practices.

I hope this book becomes an indispensable reference for all professionals dedicated to improving the quality of human relationships through CBT. May it serve as a loyal companion in your journey of learning and practice, helping to transform lives and foster healthy and fulfilling relationships.

INTRODUCTION TO COGNITIVE-BEHAVIORAL THERAPY

Cognitive-Behavioral Therapy (CBT) is a psychotherapeutic approach widely recognized for its effectiveness and versatility in treating a broad range of emotional and behavioral problems. Initially developed in the 1960s by Aaron T. Beck, CBT is based on the premise that our thoughts, emotions, and behaviors are interconnected and that modifying dysfunctional thoughts can lead to significant changes in emotions and behaviors.

Definition and History of CBT

CBT is a structured, goal-oriented, and present-focused approach that aims to identify and modify distorted thinking patterns and dysfunctional beliefs. Over the years, CBT has evolved and incorporated elements from other therapeutic approaches, becoming a modality widely used in both individual and group therapy contexts.

The Importance of CBT in Relationships

Interpersonal relationships play a crucial role in our mental health and well-being. Conflicts, communication issues, and emotional difficulties can deeply impact the quality of our relationships. CBT provides powerful tools to address these challenges, helping individuals and couples develop more effective communication skills, resolve conflicts constructively, and strengthen emotional bonds.

Objectives of This Book
This book aims to provide a comprehensive understanding of the principles and techniques of CBT as applied to relationships. Designed for psychotherapists and mental health professionals, this practical and theoretical guide covers everything from the foundations of CBT to specific interventions to enhance the quality of relationships. Through case studies, practical examples, and detailed techniques, this book seeks to empower professionals to apply CBT effectively in their clinical practice.

CHAPTER 2: ASSESSMENT AND DIAGNOSIS

Assessment Techniques in CBT
Accurate and comprehensive assessment forms the cornerstone of effective CBT interventions. Various techniques are employed to gain insights into the client's experiences:

Clinical Interviews:
These are fundamental for gathering detailed information about the client's history. Open-ended questions help understand their context, past experiences, and current issues. Creating a welcoming environment is essential for clients to feel comfortable sharing personal information.

Structured Interviews:
These follow a specific framework to ensure all relevant areas are addressed. Examples include SCID (Structured Clinical Interview for DSM Disorders) and MINI (Mini International Neuropsychiatric Interview).

Semi-Structured Interviews:
These offer therapists flexibility to delve deeper into specific areas based on the client's responses.

Questionnaires and Measurement Scales:

Standardized instruments assist in quantifying symptom severity and tracking progress. Common tools include:

Beck Depression Inventory (BDI): Measures depression severity.
Beck Anxiety Inventory (BAI): Evaluates anxiety levels.
Automatic Thoughts Questionnaire (ATQ): Identifies the frequency and intensity of negative thoughts.
Behavioral Observation:
Direct observation of a client's behavior in specific contexts provides valuable insights into their emotional reactions and interaction patterns. This is particularly helpful in group therapy or couple sessions.

Self-Monitoring:
Encouraging clients to log their daily thoughts, emotions, and behaviors can reveal recurring patterns and specific triggers. Tools like thought diaries and self-monitoring apps are often employed.

Identifying Dysfunctional Thought Patterns
Modifying dysfunctional thought patterns is central to CBT. This involves several key steps:

Automatic Thoughts:
These are immediate, often distorted, thoughts that arise in response to specific situations, contributing to emotional distress.

Examples:
"I can never do anything right."
"Nobody cares about me."
"I'm a failure."
Core Beliefs:
Deeply rooted beliefs about oneself, others, and the world. These are often formed early in life and consistently influence automatic thoughts.

Examples:
"I'm incompetent."
"People are dangerous."
"The world is unfair."
Intermediate Beliefs:
These include attitudes, rules, and assumptions derived from core beliefs, often expressed as "if…then" statements or "must/should" rules.

Examples:
"If I don't please everyone, I'll be rejected."
"I must be perfect at everything I do."
Relationship-Specific Diagnostic Tools
Evaluating relationship dynamics and identifying underlying issues require specialized techniques:

Joint Interviews:
Conducting interviews with both partners helps uncover communication problems and unresolved conflicts. Maintaining an impartial stance and fostering mutual respect are critical.

Interview Techniques:
Methods like circular questioning explore how partners influence each other's thoughts, emotions, and behaviors.

Relationship Mapping:
Tools like genograms and relationship maps help visualize family connections and identify dysfunctional patterns impacting the current relationship.

Genograms: Graphical representations of family structures and intergenerational behavior patterns.
Relationship Maps: Highlight alliances, conflicts, and power dynamics within a relationship.
Relationship Satisfaction Assessment:
Using specific questionnaires provides clear insights into areas

requiring attention.

Dyadic Adjustment Scale (DAS): Measures marital satisfaction across consensus, satisfaction, cohesion, and affective expression.
Relationship Quality Index (IRQ): Evaluates the overall quality of the relationship from both partners' perspectives.
Case Study: João and Maria
Background:
João and Maria, married for 10 years with two young children, have been experiencing frequent conflicts about responsibilities and finances. They report feeling disconnected and misunderstood.

Initial Interview:
During the initial session, João expressed feeling unappreciated for his work efforts and criticized for not helping enough at home. Maria felt overwhelmed by the mental and physical load of household tasks and caring for the children, feeling her efforts were unrecognized.

Assessment Tools Used:

Individual and Joint Sessions: Explored personal and shared perceptions of the relationship.
Relationship Satisfaction Questionnaire: Highlighted dissatisfaction in communication, emotional intimacy, and division of responsibilities.
Genogram Mapping: Revealed inherited dysfunctional communication patterns from their families of origin.
Self-Monitoring: Diaries identified recurring automatic thoughts and emotional reactions during conflicts.
Dysfunctional Thought Patterns Identified:

João:
Negative thoughts: "She's never satisfied with what I do."
Core belief: "I'm never good enough."

Maria:
Negative thoughts: "He doesn't care about what I do at home."
Core belief: "I'm invisible and unappreciated."
Intervention Plan:

Cognitive Restructuring:

João: Replace negative thoughts with balanced alternatives, such as "I'm doing my best, and that's enough."
Maria: Challenge feelings of unappreciation, replacing them with affirmations like "I'm valuable, and my work matters."
Assertive Communication Training:

Learned active listening and expressing needs clearly and respectfully.
Introduced "I" statements to avoid blame and foster constructive dialogue.
Conflict Management:

Problem-solving techniques for shared issues, such as financial planning and task distribution.
Scheduled regular discussions to address concerns in a safe environment.
Strengthening Emotional Bonds:

Suggested regular date nights and gratitude exercises to rebuild intimacy.
Exposure and Response Prevention:

Gradual exposure to anxiety-inducing situations to reduce sensitivity.
Introduced relaxation and mindfulness techniques for stress management.
Outcomes:
After several weeks of therapy, João and Maria reported significant improvements in communication and overall relationship

satisfaction. Conflicts reduced in frequency and intensity, and they felt more connected and understood. Cognitive restructuring helped them adopt a more positive and balanced perspective of themselves and their relationship.

Conclusion:
This case study demonstrates how CBT can effectively identify and modify dysfunctional thought patterns, improve communication, and resolve conflicts in relationships. By following a structured and evidence-based approach, João and Maria transformed their relationship, achieving greater harmony and fulfillment.

CHAPTER 3: COGNITIVE TECHNIQUES

Cognitive Restructuring
Cognitive restructuring is a central technique in Cognitive Behavioral Therapy (CBT), aiming to identify and modify negative automatic thoughts and dysfunctional beliefs. This process follows several defined steps:

Identifying Automatic Thoughts:
The client is encouraged to recognize negative thoughts that arise automatically in specific situations. This can be done through thought records, where the client notes their thoughts, emotions, and associated situations.

Example:
João thinks: "I never do anything right" after a mistake at work. Using a thought record, he writes down the situation (a specific mistake), his emotional reaction (sadness), and the associated thought.

Challenging Automatic Thoughts:
Negative automatic thoughts are questioned by analyzing evidence for and against them, as well as considering alternative explanations.

Example:
João is encouraged to recall moments of success at work to challenge the thought, "I never do anything right."

Replacing with Functional Thoughts:
The client learns to replace dysfunctional thoughts with more realistic and balanced versions, often using Socratic questioning.

Example:
João replaces "I never do anything right" with "I made a mistake, but I've had many achievements at work before, and I can overcome this too."

Challenging Automatic Thoughts
Several tools are used to challenge automatic thoughts:

Thought Records:
Help identify patterns by noting negative thoughts, the context in which they arose, emotions, and associated behaviors.

Example:
Maria records thoughts of feeling "invisible" in situations where she expects recognition, increasing awareness of this pattern.

Cognitive Reassessment Techniques:
Encourage the client to consider different scenarios, such as the worst, the best, and the most likely outcome.

Example:
Maria revisits situations where she felt invisible and evaluates: "Is there another explanation for the lack of recognition other than that I am irrelevant?"

Problem-Solving Techniques
These techniques help address specific challenges in various areas, especially in relationships. Steps include:

Identifying the Problem:
Clearly define the problem and break it into smaller parts.
Generating Solutions:
Brainstorm possible solutions without immediate judgment.
Evaluating Options:
Analyze the pros and cons of each solution.
Choosing and Implementing:
Develop and apply an action plan.
Evaluating Results:
Monitor outcomes and adjust as needed.
Practical Example:
João and Maria face challenges in dividing household chores. After identifying the problem, they discuss solutions like a task schedule and, after evaluating options, implement the schedule with regular reviews.

Case Study: Paulo and Ana
Background:
Paulo and Ana have been together for eight years but face communication difficulties and conflicts over the lack of quality time in their relationship.

Identified Problems:

Paulo thinks: "Ana doesn't love me anymore," due to the little time they spend together.
Ana believes: "Paulo doesn't understand my responsibilities."
Interventions:

Cognitive Restructuring:

Paulo: Identifies evidence that Ana still shows affection through small gestures.
Ana: Acknowledges that Paulo has legitimate concerns and that communication can improve.

Challenging Automatic Thoughts:
Both use thought records to identify and work on negative patterns, reducing emotional intensity.

Problem-Solving:
Together, they develop a weekly schedule for couple activities and align expectations about quality time.

Case Results
After several weeks of therapy:

Paulo and Ana reported significant improvements in communication and emotional connection.
Cognitive restructuring helped them develop more balanced and positive perspectives about their relationship.
Problem-solving techniques provided practical tools to address future challenges.
Conclusion:
This case study demonstrates how CBT cognitive techniques can transform dysfunctional thought patterns, improve communication, and resolve conflicts in relationships. Applied consistently, these tools help clients build healthier and more satisfying connections.

CHAPTER 4: BEHAVIORAL TECHNIQUES

Social Skills Training
Social skills training is an essential technique in Cognitive Behavioral Therapy (CBT), helping clients develop more effective behaviors in their social interactions. This includes communication skills, assertiveness, and empathy.

Effective Communication:
Teaching clients to express their thoughts and feelings clearly and respectfully is fundamental. Techniques such as using "I statements" (e.g., "I feel..." instead of "You always...") help avoid accusations and promote positive communication. It is also important to practice active listening, where the client fully concentrates on what the other person is saying without interrupting.

Assertiveness:
Helping clients stand up for their rights assertively without being passive or aggressive. Role-playing techniques and behavioral rehearsals are often used to practice these skills in a safe environment. Assertiveness enables individuals to express their needs and desires clearly and directly while respecting others' rights.

Empathy:
Developing the ability to understand and share others' feelings is crucial for healthy relationships. Empathy exercises may include role-reversal practices and reflecting on the emotions and experiences of the partner.

Practical Example: Paulo and Ana, from the previous case study, participated in role-playing sessions to practice assertive communication. Paulo learned to express his needs without guilt, while Ana worked on active listening, recognizing and validating Paulo's feelings.

Exposure and Response Prevention (ERP)
Exposure and response prevention (ERP) is a technique used to reduce anxiety by gradually exposing the client to feared situations without allowing them to engage in avoidance or compulsive behaviors.

Gradual Exposure:
Encouraging the client to face anxiety-provoking situations in a gradual and controlled manner, starting with less threatening situations and progressing to more challenging ones. Exposure can be conducted both in vivo (in real life) and in imagination (imaginary exposure).

Response Prevention:
Teaching the client to resist avoidance or compulsive behaviors while confronting the feared situation. This helps reduce long-term anxiety and increases the client's confidence in managing difficult situations.

Practical Example: Maria experienced significant social anxiety and avoided family events. The therapist developed a hierarchy of feared situations, starting with small family gatherings. Over time, Maria was able to attend larger events without avoidance.

Relaxation and Mindfulness Techniques

Relaxation and mindfulness techniques are fundamental for helping clients reduce stress and improve overall well-being. These techniques include:

Progressive Muscle Relaxation:

This involves tensing and relaxing different muscle groups to reduce physical tension and promote calmness. Clients are instructed to tense a muscle group for a few seconds and then release the tension, observing the difference between the tense and relaxed states.

Breathing Exercises:

Techniques such as deep and controlled breathing, like diaphragmatic breathing, help reduce anxiety and promote relaxation. Clients are taught to inhale deeply through the nose, hold their breath for a few seconds, and exhale slowly through the mouth.

Mindfulness:

Mindfulness practices, such as mindfulness meditation, help clients focus on the present and accept their thoughts and feelings without judgment. Exercises may include observing the breath, practicing body scans, and guided meditations.

Practical Example: João and Maria participated in mindfulness training sessions where they learned mindful meditation. This helped them cope with daily stress and improved their ability to communicate calmly and effectively during conflicts.

Case Study Example
Case: Lucas and Clara

Couple's History: Lucas and Clara have been together for six years and have recently faced difficulties due to Lucas's anxiety in social situations and Clara's work-related stress.

Intervention:

Social Skills Training:

Lucas: Participated in role-playing sessions to improve his communication skills and learn to be more assertive in social interactions. He practiced expressing his thoughts and feelings clearly and directly while respecting others' feelings and needs.
Clara: Learned empathy and validation techniques to support Lucas in his struggles with social anxiety. She also practiced active listening, fully focusing on what Lucas was saying and responding empathetically.
Exposure and Response Prevention (ERP):

Lucas developed a hierarchy of anxiety-provoking social situations and began with gradual exposures. He started with less intimidating situations, such as small gatherings with close friends, and gradually progressed to larger social events. Over time, he was able to attend larger events without avoidance or safety behaviors.
During the exposure process, Lucas was encouraged to resist avoidance behaviors and focus on breathing and relaxation techniques to manage his anxiety.
Relaxation and Mindfulness Techniques:

Clara learned progressive muscle relaxation and breathing exercises to cope with work-related stress. She practiced these techniques daily and particularly before stressful situations.
Both participated in mindfulness sessions to improve their connection and reduce stress in their relationship. They practiced mindfulness meditation together, which increased their awareness of their thoughts and feelings and promoted calmer and more effective communication.
Results:
Lucas reported a significant reduction in social anxiety and

greater confidence in social situations. Clara managed her work stress more effectively and felt more emotionally connected to Lucas. Both reported improvements in communication and overall relationship satisfaction. The relaxation and mindfulness techniques also helped promote a sense of calm and well-being in their relationship.

CHAPTER 5: SPECIFIC INTERVENTIONS FOR RELATIONSHIPS

Assertive Communication
Assertive communication is fundamental to the health of any relationship. It involves expressing thoughts, feelings, and needs clearly and directly while respecting the rights of others. Several techniques can promote assertive communication:

Use of "I" Statements:
Teaching clients to use "I" statements instead of "You" statements can help reduce defensiveness. For example, instead of saying, "You never listen to me," the client might say, "I feel ignored when I'm not heard."

Active Listening:
Instructing clients to practice active listening, which involves fully paying attention to what the other person is saying, reflecting back what was said, and avoiding interruptions.

Constructive Feedback:
Encouraging the provision of constructive feedback that is specific, behavior-oriented, and offered with the intention of helping the other person improve.

Practical Example: During a session, João and Maria practiced the "active listening" technique. João shared his work-related frustrations while Maria reflected back what he said, acknowledged his feelings, and avoided interrupting. This helped create an environment of mutual understanding and reduced tension between them.

Conflict Management
Conflict management is a crucial skill for maintaining healthy relationships. Conflicts inevitably arise, but how they are handled determines their impact on the relationship. Specific techniques include:

Identifying Triggers:
Helping clients recognize the triggers that lead to conflict and understand the underlying emotions.

Problem-Solving Techniques:
Engaging clients in structured problem-solving processes, including clearly defining the problem, brainstorming solutions, evaluating options, and choosing a viable solution.

Developing Agreements:
Facilitating the creation of agreements between partners on how to handle future conflicts. This might include rules for discussing issues, such as taking breaks when necessary and avoiding accusations.

Practical Example: Paulo and Ana frequently argued about the division of household chores. In a session, the therapist helped them identify conflict triggers and develop a joint action plan. They created a weekly chore schedule and agreed to review it monthly for adjustments if needed.

Strengthening Emotional Bonds
Strengthening emotional bonds between partners is essential for the longevity and quality of the relationship. This involves

increasing intimacy, trust, and empathy between partners.

Bonding Activities:
Suggesting activities partners can do together to strengthen their connection, such as regular date nights, shared hobbies, and daily rituals of affection.

Gratitude Exercises:
Encouraging partners to regularly express gratitude toward each other. Research shows that practicing gratitude can increase relationship satisfaction.

Emotional Intimacy Techniques:
Teaching techniques to enhance emotional intimacy, such as sharing deep thoughts and feelings and engaging in meaningful conversations.

Practical Example: Lucas and Clara were encouraged to implement weekly "date nights" to strengthen their bond. Additionally, they began practicing gratitude exercises where each shared three things they were grateful for about the other daily.

Exemplary Case Study
Case: Rafael and Sofia

Couple's History: Rafael and Sofia have been together for four years and have faced challenges related to communication and conflict management. Rafael tends to shut down when frustrated, while Sofia is more confrontational.

Intervention:

Assertive Communication:

Rafael: He was taught to use "I" statements to express his feelings without blaming Sofia. He practiced saying, "I feel overwhelmed when I don't have time for myself," instead of, "You never give me space."

Sofia: She learned active listening, reflecting back what Rafael said and validating his feelings without interrupting or arguing.

Conflict Management:

They identified common triggers for their conflicts, such as schedules and responsibilities. They used problem-solving techniques to develop practical solutions, like creating a shared task list and leisure schedules.

Strengthening Emotional Bonds:

They were encouraged to dedicate weekly time for bonding activities, such as outdoor walks and cooking together. They practiced gratitude exercises where, before bedtime, each shared something positive the other did during the day.

Results: After a few weeks of therapy, Rafael and Sofia reported significant improvements in communication and conflict management. Rafael felt more understood and less overwhelmed, while Sofia appreciated Rafael's efforts to communicate more openly. Both experienced an increase in intimacy and overall relationship satisfaction.

CHAPTER 6: CLINICAL CASES AND PRACTICAL EXAMPLES

Detailed Case Studies
Case studies are valuable tools in CBT, providing practical insights into how to apply techniques in real-life situations. Let's explore some detailed cases illustrating various aspects of CBT applied to relationships.

Case 1: Marina and Ricardo

Couple's Background:
Marina and Ricardo have been married for 15 years and have three children. Recently, they have been experiencing constant conflicts regarding parenting and a lack of quality time together.

Assessment:

Individual and Joint Interviews: The therapist conducted interviews to explore their individual and shared concerns. Marina felt overwhelmed by parental responsibilities, while Ricardo felt emotionally neglected.
Couples Satisfaction Questionnaires: Both completed questionnaires that revealed low satisfaction levels in communication and emotional intimacy.
Relationship Mapping: A genogram was used to identify familial

patterns that might be influencing their current dynamics.
Intervention:

Cognitive Restructuring:
Marina: Identified automatic negative thoughts like "Ricardo doesn't care about the family" and learned to challenge them with evidence of Ricardo's positive actions.
Ricardo: Recognized beliefs such as "I'm not important to Marina" and worked on replacing them with more balanced thoughts.
Communication Techniques:
They implemented "I" statements and active listening during important conversations, reducing defensiveness and fostering mutual understanding.
Conflict Management:
They developed a weekly schedule to divide parenting responsibilities and ensure quality time together. This reduced Marina's burden and increased Ricardo's emotional connection.
Results:
After six months of therapy, Marina and Ricardo reported significant improvements in communication and relationship satisfaction. Both felt more valued and understood, and conflicts decreased in frequency and intensity.

Case 2: Carlos and Júlia

Couple's Background:
Carlos and Júlia have been together for seven years. Carlos struggles with anxiety, which negatively affects their relationship. Júlia, in turn, feels overwhelmed and unable to help.

Assessment:

Interviews and Questionnaires: Initial assessment revealed that Carlos's anxiety was primarily triggered by work situations, impacting his relationship with Júlia.
Self-Monitoring: Carlos was encouraged to track his thoughts and

emotions during episodes of anxiety to identify patterns.
Intervention:

Exposure and Response Prevention (ERP):
Carlos developed a hierarchy of anxiety-provoking situations and began with gradual exposures, such as attending small work meetings without avoidance or safety behaviors.
Relaxation Techniques:
Júlia learned progressive muscle relaxation and breathing exercises to help Carlos manage anxiety at home. They also practiced mindfulness exercises together to promote calm and connection.
Problem Solving:
Carlos and Júlia participated in problem-solving sessions to address issues contributing to Carlos's anxiety and develop strategies for managing these challenges effectively.
Results:
Carlos reported a significant reduction in anxiety and greater confidence in work situations. Júlia felt more capable of supporting Carlos and less overwhelmed. Their relationship improved in terms of communication and overall satisfaction.

Case 3: Pedro and Laura

Couple's Background:
Pedro and Laura have been married for five years and have been struggling with conflict management and a lack of emotional intimacy.

Assessment:

Joint Interviews: Revealed that Pedro frequently avoided conflicts, leading to unresolved resentments. Laura felt that Pedro was emotionally distant.
Emotional Intimacy Questionnaires: Both completed questionnaires highlighting areas for improvement in emotional

intimacy.
Intervention:

Assertive Communication:
Pedro and Laura participated in sessions to improve assertive communication skills. Pedro learned to express his feelings without fear of conflict, while Laura practiced active listening and validating Pedro's feelings.
Strengthening Emotional Bonds:
They were encouraged to dedicate weekly time for bonding activities, such as date nights and gratitude practices, where they shared positive things about each other daily.
Relaxation Techniques:
They introduced relaxation and mindfulness techniques, such as guided meditation, to reduce stress and enhance emotional connection during their time together.
Results:
Pedro and Laura reported significant improvements in communication and emotional intimacy. Pedro felt more comfortable expressing his feelings and less inclined to avoid conflicts, while Laura appreciated the increased emotional connection. Both reported greater satisfaction in their relationship.

Reflections on Clinical Practice
Challenges and Solutions:
Addressing issues such as resistance to change, reluctance to participate in exercises, and difficulties in applying techniques outside therapy sessions.
Ethics and Professionalism:
Maintaining confidentiality, mutual respect, and a safe environment for clients. Discussing common ethical dilemmas and strategies for managing them.
Professional Development:
Highlighting the importance of ongoing supervision, training, and skill development to enhance clinical practice.

Conclusion

The practical application of CBT techniques in relationships can lead to significant improvements in communication, conflict management, and emotional bonding. Case studies provide concrete examples of how these techniques can be implemented and the positive outcomes that can be achieved.

CHAPTER 7: INTERVENTION TECHNIQUES IN CRISIS SITUATIONS

Crisis Assessment and Management
Crisis situations can arise suddenly and have a significant impact on relationships. Assessing and managing crises require a careful and structured approach to help individuals cope with immediate stress and tension.

Identifying Crises:
The first step in crisis management is determining whether the current situation constitutes a crisis. This can include events such as discovering infidelity, the loss of a loved one, or a traumatic event. The therapist must assess the severity and emotional impact of the event to determine the best approach.

Safety Assessment:
Ensuring the safety of the client and those involved is crucial. In severe crises, immediate measures may be needed, such as temporarily removing the client from a risky environment or involving appropriate authorities.

Providing Immediate Support:
Immediate support includes validating the client's emotions,

active listening, and offering a safe space for the client to express feelings and concerns. Grounding techniques can help clients feel more secure and present.

Practical Example:
Laura recently discovered her partner's infidelity. During the crisis session, the therapist focused on providing immediate support by validating her feelings of betrayal and pain while assessing her emotional safety. Grounding techniques were used to help Laura feel more present and less overwhelmed by her emotions.

De-escalation Techniques
De-escalation is a process used to reduce tension and emotional intensity in crisis situations. Effective de-escalation techniques can prevent conflicts from escalating and promote calmer, more rational communication.

Staying Calm:
The therapist should maintain a calm and controlled demeanor to help reduce the client's emotional intensity. A quiet voice and open body language convey safety and confidence.

Active Listening:
Allowing the client to express concerns and feelings without interruption can help de-escalate the situation. Active listening and validating the client's emotions are essential.

Reframing and Redirecting:
Reframing the client's words in a positive light and redirecting attention to practical solutions can help reduce emotional intensity and focus on problem-solving.

Practical Example:
During a heated conflict between João and Maria over financial issues, the therapist employed de-escalation techniques by

maintaining a calm posture and encouraging both to express their concerns respectfully. By reframing João's concerns about financial security and redirecting the conversation toward practical solutions, tension was gradually reduced.

Immediate Interventions
In crisis situations, immediate interventions may be necessary to help clients stabilize their emotions and cope with the immediate impact of the event. These interventions can include:

Breathing Techniques:
Teaching the client deep breathing exercises to reduce anxiety and promote calmness. Diaphragmatic breathing is particularly effective.

Grounding Exercises:
Grounding techniques, such as using the five senses to reconnect with the present environment, help clients feel safer and more centered.

Practical Guidance:
Offering practical guidance on handling the immediate situation, such as seeking social support, using community resources, or taking legal steps if necessary.

Practical Example:
After the sudden loss of a loved one, Ricardo was in a state of shock and extreme anxiety. The therapist used deep breathing techniques and grounding exercises to help Ricardo calm down. Additionally, practical guidance was provided on seeking support from family and close friends.

Exemplary Case Study
Case: Ana and Carlos

Couple's Background:

Ana and Carlos have been together for 10 years and recently faced a crisis when Carlos unexpectedly lost his job. The job loss brought significant financial and emotional stress to the couple.

Intervention:

Crisis Assessment:
During the initial assessment, the therapist identified that Carlos was experiencing high levels of anxiety and feelings of inadequacy, while Ana was worried about financial security and the family's future.

Immediate Crisis Management:
The therapist provided immediate emotional support, validating their feelings and offering a safe space for discussion. Grounding techniques helped Carlos feel more centered.

De-escalation Techniques:
During sessions addressing heated financial conflicts, the therapist used de-escalation techniques to reduce tension. By staying calm and encouraging respectful communication, Ana and Carlos improved their dialogue.

Immediate Interventions:
Carlos was taught deep breathing techniques to manage his anxiety, while Ana was encouraged to seek support from friends and family to reduce feelings of isolation. The therapist also guided the couple on accessing community resources for temporary financial support.

Results:
After several weeks of therapy, Ana and Carlos reported a significant reduction in anxiety and improved communication. Carlos began developing a plan to pursue new job opportunities, while Ana felt more comfortable sharing her financial concerns with Carlos. The couple experienced a renewed sense of

partnership and mutual support.

By employing structured crisis management, de-escalation, and immediate interventions, therapists can help clients navigate challenging situations, stabilize emotions, and rebuild trust and communication in their relationships.

CHAPTER 8: EMOTION-FOCUSED THERAPY

Integrating CBT with Emotion-Focused Therapy (EFT)
Emotion-Focused Therapy (EFT) is a therapeutic approach centered on exploring and transforming emotional experiences. Integrating EFT with Cognitive Behavioral Therapy (CBT) can enhance therapeutic practice by combining cognitive restructuring with deep emotional work.

Principles of EFT:
EFT is grounded in the idea that emotions are fundamental to self-identity and decision-making. It emphasizes the importance of accessing, understanding, and transforming painful emotions.

Practical Application Alongside CBT:
Integrating EFT with CBT involves using emotional interventions to complement cognitive work. This may include exploring past and present emotional experiences to better understand thought and behavior patterns.

Emotional Intervention Techniques
EFT emotional intervention techniques help clients identify, express, and transform their emotions in a healthy and productive manner.

Identifying and Validating Emotions:
Assisting clients in recognizing and validating their emotions is

crucial. Therapists can use open-ended and reflective questions to help clients explore their emotional experiences.

Working with Intense Emotions:
Techniques such as experiential exploration and emotional reframing can help clients process and transform intense and painful emotions.

Practical Example:
Ana, who frequently felt rejected in her relationship, was guided to identify underlying emotions of fear and vulnerability. By validating these emotions and exploring past experiences of rejection, she was able to restructure her beliefs about self-worth and improve communication with her partner.

Addressing Emotional Reactivity
Emotional reactivity can be a significant challenge in relationships, leading to conflicts and misunderstandings. Techniques for addressing emotional reactivity include:

Emotional Regulation:
Teaching emotional regulation techniques such as deep breathing, mindfulness, and relaxation can help clients manage their emotional responses in high-tension situations.

Exploring Emotional Triggers:
Helping clients identify emotional triggers that lead to reactivity and develop strategies to handle these triggers more effectively.

Practical Example:
Carlos, who often exploded in anger during arguments, learned emotional regulation techniques and worked with his therapist to identify childhood triggers contributing to his reactivity. This enabled him to develop more controlled and constructive responses during conflicts with his partner.

Exemplary Case Study
Case: Beatriz and Paulo

Couple's Background:
Beatriz and Paulo have been together for nine years and have faced challenges due to Paulo's emotional reactivity. He struggles to control his anger, leading to frequent heated arguments.

Intervention:

Integrating EFT with CBT:
The therapist worked with Paulo to identify and validate underlying emotions of frustration and fear of rejection. CBT was employed to challenge and restructure dysfunctional beliefs fueling his anger.

Emotional Intervention Techniques:
Paulo was encouraged to explore past emotional experiences contributing to his current reactivity. Through experiential exploration, he was able to reframe these emotions and gain a deeper understanding of his feelings.

Addressing Emotional Reactivity:
Paulo learned emotional regulation techniques such as deep breathing and mindfulness to manage his anger during arguments. He also worked on identifying emotional triggers and developing strategies to handle them effectively.

Results:
After several weeks of therapy, Paulo reported a significant reduction in the intensity and frequency of his anger outbursts. Beatriz observed improved communication and Paulo's ability to respond more calmly during arguments. The couple felt more emotionally connected and experienced greater satisfaction in their relationship.

CHAPTER 9: THERAPY FOR DIVERSE RELATIONSHIPS

Adaptations for Different Types of Relationships
The diversity of relationships requires specific adaptations when applying Cognitive Behavioral Therapy (CBT). This includes considering cultural, social, and identity nuances that influence relational dynamics.

LGBTQ+ Relationships:
Working with LGBTQ+ individuals and couples involves understanding their unique challenges, such as discrimination, stigma, and identity issues. Creating a safe and inclusive space where clients can explore their concerns without judgment is essential.

Practical Example:
In a session with an LGBTQ+ couple, the therapist focused on validating their experiences of discrimination and worked on building resilience and mutual support within the relationship.

Intercultural Relationships:
Couples from different cultural backgrounds may face specific challenges, such as conflicts related to values, traditions, and cultural expectations. CBT can be adapted to address these issues by fostering communication and intercultural understanding.

Practical Example:
For an intercultural couple, the therapist facilitated conversations about cultural differences and helped them find ways to integrate their traditions harmoniously.

Law Enforcement and Military Relationships:
Individuals in high-risk professions, such as law enforcement and the military, may face unique stressors affecting their relationships. These include trauma, irregular schedules, and the need to handle high-pressure situations.

Practical Example:
In sessions, the therapist addressed the trauma experiences of a police officer and worked with the couple to develop strategies for mutual support and effective communication.

Age-Gap Relationships:
Couples with significant age differences may face social prejudice and challenges related to different life stages. CBT can help address these issues by promoting mutual understanding and acceptance of differences.

Practical Example:
For a couple with a 20-year age gap, the therapist helped identify and restructure dysfunctional beliefs related to social stigma and encouraged them to focus on their relationship's strengths.

Long-Distance Relationships:
Maintaining a long-distance relationship can be challenging due to a lack of physical proximity and the need for constant communication. CBT can help develop effective communication strategies and manage separation anxiety.

Practical Example:
The therapist helped a long-distance couple establish

communication routines, utilize technology to maintain their connection, and work on building mutual trust.

Inclusive Approaches in CBT
Creating an inclusive therapeutic environment is vital for effectively working with diverse relationships. Strategies include:

Creating a Safe Space:
Ensure the therapeutic space is welcoming and inclusive for all clients, regardless of their sexual orientation, gender identity, cultural background, or occupation. Visual signs of inclusion, such as pride flags and informational materials, can help.

Inclusive Practices:
Use respectful, inclusive language, avoid assumptions based on appearances, and ask clients directly about their preferred pronouns and how they wish to be addressed.

Cultural Sensitivity and Awareness:
Invest in ongoing education about cultural and identity-related issues. This helps therapists better understand clients' specific concerns and tailor CBT interventions accordingly.

Continuous Training:
Attend workshops and training sessions on diversity and inclusion to stay updated on best practices.

Cultural and Social Considerations:
Recognize and respect cultural and social influences shaping clients' beliefs and behaviors. Adapt CBT interventions to consider these influences for effective treatment.

Cultural Example:
In cultures valuing collectivism, therapists might focus on techniques promoting family harmony and mutual respect.

Practical Example:
With a couple of immigrants, the therapist took time to learn about their cultural backgrounds and how these influenced their expectations and relational dynamics. This allowed culturally sensitive and effective CBT adaptations.

Exemplary Case Study
Case: Thiago and Rafael

Couple's Background:
Thiago and Rafael have been together for five years and recently faced challenges related to workplace discrimination and family acceptance of their LGBTQ+ relationship.

Intervention:

Creating a Safe Space:
The therapist ensured an inclusive therapeutic environment with visual signs of LGBTQ+ support and fostered a space where Thiago and Rafael felt comfortable sharing their experiences without fear of judgment.

Validation and Resilience:
The therapist validated their experiences with discrimination and helped build resilience through self-esteem strengthening techniques and strategies for managing prejudice.

Culturally Sensitive Approach:
The therapist explored the cultural and family issues affecting Thiago and Rafael's relationship. Together, they developed strategies for communicating with their families and balancing cultural identities with LGBTQ+ identities.

Results:
Thiago and Rafael reported significant improvement in their ability to cope with discrimination and familial pressures.

They developed more open communication and strengthened mutual support, resulting in greater relationship satisfaction and stability.

CHAPTER 10: ONLINE THERAPY AND CBT

Advantages of Online Therapy in CBT
Online therapy has become an essential tool for practicing Cognitive Behavioral Therapy (CBT), particularly during pandemics and in regions with limited access to mental health services. Here are some of the main ways online therapy can benefit psychotherapists and their clients:

Enhanced Accessibility:
Online therapy enables clients in remote areas or with mobility challenges to access CBT. This is particularly relevant in large countries like Brazil, where not everyone has easy access to mental health services.

Practical Example:
A client living in a rural area can connect with a CBT specialist in a major city, receiving the same level of care as in an in-person session.

Flexible Scheduling:
Scheduling sessions outside traditional working hours can benefit both clients and therapists. This flexibility helps integrate therapy into daily routines, improving treatment adherence.

Practical Example:
A client working alternating shifts can schedule CBT sessions at

convenient times without needing to miss work.

Comfort and Privacy:
Conducting CBT sessions from the comfort of home can reduce anxiety associated with attending therapy in a clinic. It also provides a familiar and safe environment for the client.

Practical Example:
A teenager uncomfortable in a traditional office setting may benefit from online sessions where they feel more at ease expressing themselves.

CBT Techniques Applied Online
CBT can be effectively delivered online using various techniques adapted to digital platforms.

Cognitive Restructuring:
The therapist can guide the client through cognitive restructuring exercises using screen-sharing to display charts and thought records. Digital tools like online whiteboards can facilitate interaction.

Practical Example:
During a session, the therapist shares a digital whiteboard where the client notes automatic thoughts, and together they work on challenging and replacing them with more balanced thoughts.

Gradual Exposure:
Exposure and Response Prevention (ERP) can be conducted online, with the therapist guiding the client to gradually confront feared situations in a controlled and safe environment.

Practical Example:
A client with social phobia is guided through gradual exposures, starting with online simulations and progressively facing real social situations.

Thought Records:
Using digital tools, clients can maintain daily records of thoughts and emotions, which are easily shared with the therapist for analysis and discussion during sessions.

Practical Example:
Through an app, the client logs automatic thoughts and associated emotions throughout the week, allowing the therapist to review and discuss these records in the next session.

Practical Examples of Online Interventions
Case: João and Maria

Couple's Background:
João and Maria have been married for 10 years and are facing challenges related to communication and conflict management. Due to the COVID-19 pandemic, they decided to start online couples therapy.

Intervention:

Cognitive Restructuring:
The therapist used screen-sharing tools to guide João and Maria through cognitive restructuring exercises. They identified and challenged negative automatic thoughts contributing to their conflicts.

Gradual Exposure:
Maria experienced social anxiety that affected her family interactions. The therapist utilized online ERP to gradually expose her to social situations, starting with virtual interactions and progressing to in-person meetings.

Thought Records:
João and Maria were encouraged to maintain digital records of

thoughts and emotions, which they shared with the therapist before sessions. This facilitated analysis and discussion during online sessions.

Results:
After several weeks of online therapy, João and Maria reported significant improvement in communication and conflict management. Cognitive restructuring and gradual exposure helped them develop a more balanced view of themselves and their relationship, resulting in greater satisfaction and harmony.

CHAPTER 11: THERAPY FOR FAMILIES AND SUPPORT NETWORKS

Systemic Approaches in CBT

Cognitive Behavioral Therapy (CBT) can be applied not only to individuals but also to entire families and their support networks by adopting a systemic approach. This involves considering the dynamics and interactions within the family system and how they influence individual behaviors and emotions.

Working with Families:

Involving the family in therapy can help identify dysfunctional interaction patterns and promote positive changes in the family environment. CBT can be adapted to address specific issues within the family context, such as poor communication, recurring conflicts, and rigid family roles.

Practical Example:

In a family where parents and children struggle with communication, the therapist can use role-playing techniques to improve the expression of feelings and active listening.

Support Networks:

Beyond the nuclear family, support networks such as close friends and extended family members play a crucial role in individuals' mental health. CBT can include interventions that involve these support networks, fostering a more understanding and supportive environment.

Practical Example:
For a client going through a difficult time, involving close friends in therapy sessions can provide additional emotional and practical support.

Techniques for Including Support Networks
Incorporating support networks in CBT can enhance the effectiveness of treatment by providing clients with a broader supportive environment. Techniques include:

Group Sessions:
Conducting CBT group sessions can be beneficial for addressing family dynamics or interactions within the support network. These sessions allow everyone involved to express concerns and work together to find solutions.

Practical Example:
A group session with parents and teenage children can focus on improving communication and resolving conflicts related to discipline and responsibilities.

Skill Training:
Teaching communication, problem-solving, and emotional support skills to members of the support network can help create a more positive and understanding environment.

Practical Example:
A therapist can train parents in assertive communication techniques to promote open and respectful dialogue with their children.

Joint Interventions:
Involving the support network in therapeutic interventions, such

as relaxation and mindfulness practices, can increase cohesion and reduce stress within the family system.

Practical Example:
Inviting family members to participate in mindfulness sessions can help everyone cope better with stress and strengthen family bonds.

Specific Family Interventions
Several specific interventions can be applied in CBT for families to improve dynamics and resolve conflicts, including:

Family Communication:
Enhancing communication within the family is essential for resolving conflicts and strengthening relationships. Techniques such as active listening, constructive feedback, and the use of "I" statements can be taught and practiced during sessions.

Practical Example:
A family struggling to discuss emotional issues can practice using "I" statements to express feelings without blaming others, fostering more constructive dialogue.

Conflict Resolution:
Developing conflict resolution skills can help families address disagreements more effectively. Techniques such as mediation and negotiation can be taught to promote collaborative solutions.

Practical Example:
During a family session, the therapist can facilitate a structured discussion where each member presents concerns, and they work together to find solutions that meet everyone's needs.

Strengthening Family Bonds:
Activities that strengthen emotional bonds within the family are essential for creating a supportive and understanding

environment. These can include planned family activities, rituals, and quality time together.

Practical Example:
Planning weekly family activities, such as game nights or outdoor outings, can help strengthen relationships and foster a positive atmosphere.

Case Study Example
Case: The Silva Family

Family Background:
The Silva family consists of two parents, Paulo and Ana, and their three children, Lucas, Mariana, and Pedro. They have recently been experiencing frequent conflicts related to disciplining the children and communication issues among family members.

Intervention:

Group Sessions:
The therapist conducted CBT group sessions with the entire family. During these sessions, each member had the opportunity to express their concerns and feelings in a safe and structured environment.

Role-playing techniques were used to practice communication skills and resolve simulated conflicts.
Skill Training:

Paulo and Ana received training in assertive communication and problem-solving techniques. They learned to use "I" statements and provide constructive feedback.
The children were taught how to express their feelings respectfully and actively listen to their parents and siblings.
Joint Interventions:

The family participated in mindfulness sessions to reduce stress and promote a calmer and more understanding environment.

Weekly family activities, such as game nights and outings, were planned to strengthen emotional bonds and create moments of quality time together.

Results:

After several weeks of therapy, the Silva family reported significant improvements in communication and a reduction in conflicts. Paulo and Ana successfully applied assertive communication and problem-solving techniques, fostering a more harmonious environment. The children felt more understood and supported, resulting in a more positive and cohesive family dynamic.

CHAPTER 12: GROUP THERAPY IN RELATIONSHIPS

Benefits of Group Therapy

Group therapy offers unique advantages that are not easily replicated in individual or couples' sessions. In a group setting, participants can share experiences, provide mutual support, and learn from each other's journeys. Key benefits include:

Support and Validation:

Being part of a group allows individuals to receive emotional support and validation from others facing similar challenges. This can be particularly powerful as group members feel understood and less isolated.

Practical Example:

In a support group for couples, participants share struggles with communication and receive empathy and practical suggestions from other couples who have faced similar situations.

Constructive Feedback:

The group environment provides opportunities for participants to receive constructive feedback from multiple perspectives, helping them gain new insights into their behaviors and thought patterns.

Practical Example:

During a group session, a participant shares a conflict situation with their partner and receives useful feedback from other members on handling it more effectively.

Modeling and Observational Learning:
Group members can learn new skills by observing how others cope with their challenges. This includes communication skills, conflict resolution techniques, and coping strategies.

Practical Example:
A participant struggling with assertiveness observes another group member practicing assertive communication and applies these techniques in their own life.

Group Dynamics and Interactions
The effectiveness of group therapy largely depends on the dynamics and interactions among group members. A skilled therapist can facilitate these interactions to create a safe and productive environment.

Establishing Group Rules:
At the beginning of sessions, it's important to establish clear rules to ensure that all members feel safe and respected. This may include guidelines on confidentiality, mutual respect, and active listening.

Practical Example:
In the first session, the therapist explains confidentiality rules and encourages participants to listen without interruptions when someone is sharing.

Creating a Safe Environment:
Building a welcoming, non-judgmental space is crucial for group members to feel comfortable sharing their experiences. The therapist models this behavior and encourages group members to do the same.

Practical Example:
The therapist begins each session with an icebreaker activity to help participants feel connected and comfortable sharing.

Facilitating Interactions:
The therapist guides discussions to ensure that everyone has an opportunity to speak and that interactions remain productive and focused on the group's goals.

Practical Example:
During a session, the therapist uses open-ended questions to encourage participation and redirects the conversation if it strays from key topics.

Group Facilitation Techniques
Several techniques can be used to facilitate effective group therapy, ensuring engagement and fostering positive dynamics.

Sharing Rounds:
A common technique is a sharing round, where each group member has the opportunity to speak about their experiences and feelings without interruptions. This ensures that everyone has a chance to express themselves.

Practical Example:
At the start of each session, the therapist leads a sharing round where each member briefly discusses a recent challenge or personal achievement.

Role-Playing Exercises:
Role-playing can be a powerful tool for practicing new skills and coping strategies in a safe environment. Group members can take on different roles and receive constructive feedback.

Practical Example:

In a session focused on communication, the therapist organizes a role-playing exercise where participants practice assertive communication in conflict scenarios.

Small Group Discussions:
Dividing the group into smaller subgroups for discussions can encourage active participation from all members. These subgroups can later share their insights with the larger group.

Practical Example:
The therapist splits participants into smaller groups to discuss conflict resolution strategies and then reconvenes the larger group to share their ideas.

Case Study Example
Case: Couples Support Group

Group Background:
A support group for couples was created to help them address challenges related to communication, intimacy, and conflict management. The group comprised five couples, each with unique experiences and difficulties.

Intervention:

Establishing Group Rules:
In the first session, the therapist established clear guidelines on confidentiality, mutual respect, and active listening. Couples were encouraged to share openly without fear of judgment.

Creating a Safe Environment:
The therapist started each session with an opening activity to build a welcoming atmosphere. This included gratitude exercises where each couple shared something positive about their partner.

Facilitating Interactions:

Throughout the sessions, the therapist used open-ended questions to encourage participation and maintained a structured sharing round to ensure everyone had an opportunity to speak.

Role-Playing Exercises:
Several sessions included role-playing exercises where couples practiced assertive communication and conflict resolution in simulated scenarios. This allowed them to experiment with new skills in a safe setting.

Results:
After several weeks of group therapy, couples reported significant improvements in communication and conflict management. They felt supported by the group and learned new strategies by observing and practicing with others. The positive group dynamic fostered an environment of growth and healing for all participants.

CHAPTER 13: RESEARCH AND SCIENTIFIC EVIDENCE

The Importance of Research in CBT
Cognitive Behavioral Therapy (CBT) is an evidence-based approach, meaning its effectiveness is supported by extensive scientific research. The significance of research in CBT includes:

Validation of Methods:
Research provides data that validate the methods and techniques used in CBT, ensuring that interventions are effective for a wide range of disorders and issues.

Development of New Techniques:
Ongoing research enables the development and refinement of new techniques and interventions, adapting CBT to emerging client needs.

Evidence-Based Practice:
Integrating research into clinical practice ensures therapists use the most up-to-date and effective interventions, enhancing the quality of client care.

Studies on CBT Effectiveness in Relationships
Numerous studies have demonstrated the effectiveness of CBT in improving relationship quality and resolving interpersonal

conflicts. Below are examples of research highlighting this effectiveness:

Meta-Analyses and Systematic Reviews:
Many meta-analyses and systematic reviews conclude that CBT is effective in addressing relationship issues, including couples therapy and family therapy. These studies show that CBT improves communication, enhances relational satisfaction, and reduces conflicts.

Practical Example:
A meta-analysis conducted by researchers at Oxford University found that CBT significantly improved marital satisfaction and conflict resolution.

Case-Controlled Studies:
Case-controlled studies comparing CBT to other therapeutic approaches have shown that CBT is as effective, if not more so, in improving interpersonal relationships.

Practical Example:
A randomized controlled study published in the Journal of Family Psychology compared CBT to psychodynamic therapy for couples and found that CBT was more effective in reducing symptoms of anxiety and depression associated with marital conflicts.

Long-Term Research:
Long-term studies tracking couples and families over several years demonstrate that the benefits of CBT are lasting. These studies indicate that skills learned in CBT continue to be applied and improve relationships over time.

Practical Example:
A longitudinal study conducted by the University of California followed couples who underwent CBT and found that they continued to report higher levels of marital satisfaction five years

after completing therapy.

Implementing Evidence-Based Practices

To ensure CBT practice is evidence-based, therapists must integrate research findings into their daily work. This can be achieved in several ways:

Continuous Education:

Attending workshops, conferences, and training courses on CBT to stay updated with the latest findings and evidence-based practices.

Practical Example:

A therapist attends an annual CBT conference to learn about new techniques and recent studies applicable to their clinical practice.

Reading Scientific Articles:

Keeping informed about the latest research by reading articles published in reputable scientific journals, such as Journal of Cognitive Psychotherapy and Cognitive Behaviour Therapy.

Practical Example:

Regularly reviewing summaries of recent studies helps therapists incorporate new evidence into their intervention techniques.

Continuous Outcome Assessment:

Monitoring and evaluating client outcomes ensures that interventions are effective and allows adjustments as needed.

Practical Example:

Using satisfaction questionnaires and progress scales regularly to measure intervention effectiveness and make adjustments based on client feedback.

Case Study Example
Case: Ana and Lucas

Couple's Background:
Ana and Lucas have been together for eight years and sought therapy due to recurring conflicts about parenting and communication. They chose CBT due to its strong scientific support.

Intervention:

Evidence-Based Techniques:
The therapist used research-validated techniques, such as cognitive restructuring and assertive communication techniques, to help Ana and Lucas identify and modify dysfunctional thoughts contributing to conflicts.

Incorporation of Research:
During therapy, the therapist shared study findings demonstrating CBT's effectiveness in improving communication and reducing conflicts, which increased the couple's motivation to engage with the proposed interventions.

Ongoing Monitoring:
Ana and Lucas's progress was regularly monitored using satisfaction questionnaires and communication assessment scales. This allowed the therapist to adjust techniques as necessary to ensure optimal outcomes.

Results:
After six months of therapy, Ana and Lucas reported significant improvements in communication and conflict resolution. They felt more connected and satisfied in their relationship, and the skills learned during CBT continued to benefit the couple in the long term.

CHAPTER 14: ETHICS AND PROFESSIONALISM IN CBT

Ethical Principles in CBT Practice

Ethical principles are fundamental to the practice of Cognitive Behavioral Therapy (CBT). These principles ensure therapists provide high-quality care and respect clients' rights and dignity. Key ethical principles include:

Confidentiality:

Protecting client privacy is crucial. Information shared during therapy sessions must remain confidential, except in cases where there is a risk of harm to the client or others.

Practical Example:

A therapist assures clients that their personal information and session discussions will not be shared without explicit consent, unless in an emergency situation.

Informed Consent:

Before beginning treatment, clients must be informed about the methods, goals, risks, and benefits of CBT. They must provide free and informed consent to participate in therapy.

Practical Example:
In the initial session, the therapist explains CBT in detail, how it works, and answers any client questions before proceeding.

Competence:
Therapists should provide services only within the scope of their training and expertise. Continuous professional development is essential to ensure practices are up-to-date.

Practical Example:
A CBT therapist specializing in anxiety disorders avoids treating addiction issues unless they have the necessary training.

Avoiding Harm:
Therapists must take all possible measures to prevent harm to their clients, ensuring that interventions are appropriate and effective.

Practical Example:
A therapist avoids using overly intense exposure techniques with clients unprepared for them to prevent retraumatization or increased anxiety.

Continuous Professional Development
CBT practice, like any other health field, requires ongoing professional development to ensure therapists stay updated on the latest research and techniques. Key methods for continuous development include:

Supervision:
Regular supervision with an experienced therapist helps refine skills and provides constructive feedback on clinical practice.

Practical Example:
A novice CBT therapist meets weekly with a supervisor to discuss cases, review intervention techniques, and address ethical

dilemmas.

Trainings and Workshops:
Attending training sessions and workshops is an effective way to learn new techniques, deepen knowledge in specific areas, and stay updated on the latest research.

Practical Example:
A therapist attends a weekend workshop on CBT for eating disorders to expand their skills in this area.

Reading and Research:
Staying informed about the latest research and practices through books, scientific articles, and specialized journals is crucial.

Practical Example:
Regularly reading journals like Behavior Therapy and Cognitive Therapy and Research helps therapists stay updated on CBT advancements.

Maintaining Clinical Competence
Maintaining clinical competence involves continuous practice of therapeutic skills and reflection on one's practice. Strategies include:

Critical Reflection:
Reflecting on sessions and techniques used helps identify areas for improvement and reinforce effective strategies.

Practical Example:
After each session, a therapist writes reflective notes on what worked well and what could be handled differently.

Study Groups:
Joining study groups with other therapists provides opportunities to discuss cases, share knowledge, and learn from colleagues'

experiences.

Practical Example:
A monthly CBT study group discusses recent articles, complex cases, and new techniques to enrich clinical practice.

Performance Evaluation:
Soliciting client feedback and conducting regular performance reviews provide valuable insights into the effectiveness of interventions and client satisfaction.

Practical Example:
A therapist uses feedback questionnaires at the end of each therapy cycle to assess client satisfaction and identify areas for improvement.

Case Study Example
Case: Carla, CBT Therapist

Therapist Background:
Carla is a CBT therapist with five years of experience. She is committed to continually improving her skills and maintaining ethical and professional practice.

Professional Development Practices:

Supervision:
Carla attends monthly supervision sessions with an experienced therapist to discuss complex cases and receive feedback on her interventions.

Trainings and Workshops:
Carla regularly attends workshops and conferences on CBT. Recently, she completed an intensive course on CBT for post-traumatic stress disorder (PTSD).

Reading and Research:
Carla subscribes to several scientific journals and dedicates weekly time to reading articles and research, helping her incorporate evidence-based techniques into her clinical practice.

Critical Reflection:
After each session, Carla writes reflective notes on what worked well and areas for improvement, using these insights to adjust her approaches in future sessions.

Study Groups:
Carla is part of a monthly CBT study group, where therapists discuss cases, share experiences, and review new research together.

Results:
Through her dedication to continuous professional development and ethical practice, Carla consistently delivers high-quality care to her clients. Her clients report high levels of satisfaction and positive treatment outcomes, reflecting Carla's commitment to excellence in CBT practice.

CHAPTER 15: SELF-CARE FOR PSYCHOTHERAPISTS

The Importance of Self-Care for Mental Health Professionals
Self-care is essential for all mental health professionals, including psychotherapists practicing Cognitive Behavioral Therapy (CBT). Taking care of oneself not only benefits the therapist but also improves the quality of care provided to clients. Key benefits of self-care include:

Burnout Prevention:
Burnout is a common risk for mental health professionals due to the emotionally demanding nature of their work. Regular self-care practices can help prevent emotional exhaustion and maintain the therapist's mental health.

Practical Example:
A therapist establishes a daily routine of meditation and physical exercise to reduce stress and promote overall well-being.

Improved Quality of Care:
Therapists who practice self-care are more effective in their work, as they are mentally and emotionally balanced. This leads to better client outcomes.

Practical Example:

A therapist who regularly practices relaxation techniques is more present and attentive during sessions, offering more effective support to clients.

Work-Life Balance:
Maintaining a healthy balance between professional and personal life is crucial for mental health and well-being. This includes dedicating time to leisure activities, hobbies, and personal relationships.

Practical Example:
Scheduling regular recreational activities such as outdoor walks, artistic hobbies, or social gatherings helps maintain a healthy balance.

Self-Care Strategies
Therapists can adopt several strategies to promote self-care and maintain their mental health:

Relaxation Techniques:
Practicing relaxation techniques like meditation, yoga, and deep breathing can help reduce stress and promote calmness.

Practical Example:
Including a 10-minute guided meditation session at the start or end of the workday can help reduce stress and foster relaxation.

Physical Exercise:
Maintaining a regular exercise routine is essential for physical and mental health. Activities such as walking, running, swimming, or dancing can release endorphins and improve mood.

Practical Example:
Setting aside time for a morning walk or a light jog is an excellent way to start the day with energy and positivity.

Healthy Eating:
Following a balanced and nutritious diet positively impacts mental health and overall well-being. Consuming a variety of healthy foods helps sustain energy levels and improve focus.

Practical Example:
Planning meals rich in fruits, vegetables, lean proteins, and whole grains can contribute to physical and mental health.

Supervision and Professional Support:
Regular supervision and seeking professional support provide valuable perspectives and help address specific challenges in clinical work.

Practical Example:
Participating in a monthly supervision group with other therapists provides emotional support, constructive feedback, and learning opportunities.

Self-Compassion and Reflection:
Practicing self-compassion and reflection helps therapists cope with feelings of inadequacy or stress. This involves treating oneself with the same kindness and understanding extended to clients.

Practical Example:
Keeping a gratitude journal and writing reflections can cultivate a positive attitude and self-compassion.

Work-Life Balance
Maintaining a healthy balance between professional and personal life is critical for therapists' well-being. This can be achieved through various practices:

Setting Boundaries:
Establishing clear boundaries between work and personal life is

essential. This includes specific working hours, avoiding work at home, and reserving time for personal activities.

Practical Example:
Setting a fixed time to end work and dedicating evenings to personal activities helps maintain a healthy balance.

Rest and Recovery Time:
Ensuring adequate time for rest and recovery is crucial for maintaining energy and mental health. This includes proper sleep and regular breaks during the workday.

Practical Example:
Planning regular breaks throughout the day and ensuring quality sleep helps maintain energy levels and prevent burnout.

Leisure Activities and Hobbies:
Dedicating time to leisure activities and hobbies can provide relaxation and enjoyment, helping counterbalance the stress of clinical work.

Practical Example:
Engaging in a painting class, playing a musical instrument, or participating in sports can offer a revitalizing break from the work routine.

Case Study Example
Case: Laura, CBT Therapist

Therapist Background:
Laura is a CBT therapist with ten years of experience. She recently began experiencing signs of burnout due to high work demands and insufficient self-care.

Self-Care Strategies Implemented:

Relaxation Techniques:
Laura incorporated daily meditation and yoga sessions into her morning routine, helping her start the day calmly and balanced.

Physical Exercise:
She began running three times a week, which improved her mood and energy levels.

Healthy Eating:
Laura adjusted her diet to include more nutritious foods while reducing caffeine and sugar intake.

Supervision and Professional Support:
She attended monthly supervision with a colleague, providing emotional support and opportunities for clinical reflection.

Self-Compassion and Reflection:
Laura kept a gratitude journal, recording three positive things each day to cultivate self-compassion and positivity.

Setting Boundaries:
She established specific working hours, avoided taking work home, and dedicated evenings to personal and family activities.

Results:
After implementing these self-care strategies, Laura reported significant improvements in her overall well-being and a reduction in burnout symptoms. She felt more balanced and energized, which enhanced her effectiveness in supporting her clients.

CHAPTER 16: THE FUTURE OF CBT IN RELATIONSHIPS

Emerging Trends in CBT

As Cognitive Behavioral Therapy (CBT) continues to evolve, several emerging trends are shaping the future of this therapeutic approach, particularly in the context of relationships. Some of these trends include:

Integration with Digital Technologies:

The use of digital technologies in CBT is rapidly expanding, including mental health apps, teletherapy platforms, and online CBT programs. These tools offer broader and more convenient access to therapy.

Practical Example:

Apps offering daily CBT exercises, mood tracking, and educational resources can complement traditional therapy sessions, providing additional support between appointments.

Mindfulness-Based CBT:

The integration of mindfulness practices in CBT has shown promising results. Mindfulness helps clients develop greater awareness and acceptance of their thoughts and emotions, promoting self-regulation and emotional well-being.

Practical Example:
Mindfulness-Based Cognitive Therapy (MBCT) combines CBT with mindfulness techniques to help clients manage negative automatic thoughts and prevent depression relapse.

Personalization of CBT:
Personalized CBT approaches are gaining prominence, where interventions are tailored to the unique needs and characteristics of each client. This includes considering factors such as personality, learning preferences, and cultural background.

Practical Example:
Conducting detailed initial assessments to develop personalized treatment plans that address the client's specific challenges and goals.

New Approaches and Techniques
Advances in research and clinical practice are leading to the development of new approaches and techniques to enhance CBT's effectiveness in relationships.

Compassion-Focused Therapy (CFT):
CFT combines CBT principles with compassion practices to help clients develop self-compassion and reduce self-criticism. This can be particularly beneficial in relationships, where self-compassion can improve empathy and mutual understanding.

Practical Example:
Introducing compassion exercises during CBT sessions to help clients practice self-compassion and compassion for others, fostering healthier relationships.

Acceptance and Commitment Therapy (ACT):
ACT, a form of CBT, emphasizes accepting emotional experiences and committing to actions aligned with personal values. This helps clients better manage conflicts and make healthier

decisions in their relationships.

Practical Example:
Using ACT techniques to help clients accept difficult emotions and commit to actions that promote meaningful and satisfying relationships.

Dialectical Behavior Therapy (DBT):
Originally developed for treating borderline personality disorder, DBT has been adapted to address various relationship problems. It combines CBT techniques with emotional regulation, distress tolerance, and mindfulness skills.

Practical Example:
Integrating DBT skills modules into CBT sessions to help clients improve emotional regulation and effective communication in their relationships.

Reflections on the Evolution of Practice
As CBT continues to evolve, it is essential to reflect on its impact and future potential in relationship therapy.

Positive Impact of CBT:
CBT has proven to be an effective approach for improving communication, resolving conflicts, and strengthening emotional bonds in relationships. Ongoing practice and the development of evidence-based techniques will further enhance its outcomes.

Practical Example:
Continuous studies on CBT's effectiveness in various relationship contexts refine and validate interventions, ensuring they remain relevant and effective.

Transformative Potential:
CBT has the potential to transform how people understand and

manage their relationships. By providing practical and evidence-based tools, CBT empowers individuals to develop healthy and fulfilling relationships.

Practical Example:
Implementing CBT-based prevention programs in schools and communities can educate individuals early about healthy relationship skills, fostering a more connected and empathetic society.

Future Visions:
The future of CBT in relationships involves the continued integration of new research, technologies, and therapeutic approaches. Collaboration among researchers, clinicians, and educators will be key to advancing CBT practice.

Practical Example:
Establishing partnerships between universities, mental health clinics, and community organizations to conduct collaborative research and develop innovative training programs.

Case Study Example
Case: Marcos and Daniela

Couple's Background:
Marcos and Daniela have been married for 12 years and have faced challenges related to communication and stress management. They decided to seek therapy to strengthen their relationship and learn new skills to address their challenges.

Intervention:

Mindfulness Integration:
The therapist introduced mindfulness practices during CBT sessions to help Marcos and Daniela develop greater awareness and acceptance of their thoughts and emotions. They practiced

breathing exercises and meditation together.

Personalized CBT:
The therapist conducted a detailed initial assessment to develop a personalized treatment plan. Interventions were tailored to Marcos and Daniela's specific needs and characteristics, including their learning preferences and cultural background.

New Therapeutic Approaches:

Acceptance and Commitment Therapy (ACT) techniques were used to help them accept difficult emotions and commit to actions promoting a meaningful relationship.
Compassion-Focused Therapy (CFT) was introduced to help them develop self-compassion and compassion for each other, enhancing empathy and mutual understanding.
Results:
After several weeks of therapy, Marcos and Daniela reported significant improvements in communication and stress management. Mindfulness practices, along with ACT and CFT techniques, helped them develop a more balanced and compassionate view of themselves and their relationship. They felt more connected and satisfied, resulting in a stronger and more resilient partnership.

Final Thoughts
Being well within oneself is the foundation upon which a relationship therapist builds their work. Much like a sturdy tree with deep, healthy roots, a therapist who nurtures their well-being can weather emotional storms and provide robust support to clients seeking guidance.

Authenticity and empathy—the cornerstones of the therapeutic relationship—stem from internal balance. A therapist who practices self-reflection, self-compassion, and a balanced lifestyle can connect genuinely with clients, listen attentively, and respond wisely.

Without personal stability, therapists risk emotional fatigue and burnout. Regular self-care practices, professional supervision, and time away from work are crucial to maintaining the equilibrium necessary for effective therapy.

Ultimately, a therapist's well-being is both a personal benefit and a professional responsibility. By prioritizing self-care, therapists can provide a stable and transformative space where relationships can flourish, and healing can occur. Remember: to care for others, one must first care for oneself.

CHAPTER 16: THE FUTURE OF CBT IN RELATIONSHIPS

Emerging Trends in CBT

As Cognitive Behavioral Therapy (CBT) continues to evolve, several emerging trends are shaping the future of this therapeutic approach, particularly in the context of relationships. Some of these trends include:

Integration with Digital Technologies:

The use of digital technologies in CBT is rapidly expanding, including mental health apps, teletherapy platforms, and online CBT programs. These tools offer broader and more convenient access to therapy.

Practical Example:

Apps offering daily CBT exercises, mood tracking, and educational resources can complement traditional therapy sessions, providing additional support between appointments.

Mindfulness-Based CBT:

The integration of mindfulness practices in CBT has shown promising results. Mindfulness helps clients develop greater awareness and acceptance of their thoughts and emotions, promoting self-regulation and emotional well-being.

Practical Example:
Mindfulness-Based Cognitive Therapy (MBCT) combines CBT with mindfulness techniques to help clients manage negative automatic thoughts and prevent depression relapse.

Personalization of CBT:
Personalized CBT approaches are gaining prominence, where interventions are tailored to the unique needs and characteristics of each client. This includes considering factors such as personality, learning preferences, and cultural background.

Practical Example:
Conducting detailed initial assessments to develop personalized treatment plans that address the client's specific challenges and goals.

New Approaches and Techniques
Advances in research and clinical practice are leading to the development of new approaches and techniques to enhance CBT's effectiveness in relationships.

Compassion-Focused Therapy (CFT):
CFT combines CBT principles with compassion practices to help clients develop self-compassion and reduce self-criticism. This can be particularly beneficial in relationships, where self-compassion can improve empathy and mutual understanding.

Practical Example:
Introducing compassion exercises during CBT sessions to help clients practice self-compassion and compassion for others, fostering healthier relationships.

Acceptance and Commitment Therapy (ACT):
ACT, a form of CBT, emphasizes accepting emotional experiences and committing to actions aligned with personal values. This helps clients better manage conflicts and make healthier

decisions in their relationships.

Practical Example:
Using ACT techniques to help clients accept difficult emotions and commit to actions that promote meaningful and satisfying relationships.

Dialectical Behavior Therapy (DBT):
Originally developed for treating borderline personality disorder, DBT has been adapted to address various relationship problems. It combines CBT techniques with emotional regulation, distress tolerance, and mindfulness skills.

Practical Example:
Integrating DBT skills modules into CBT sessions to help clients improve emotional regulation and effective communication in their relationships.

Reflections on the Evolution of Practice
As CBT continues to evolve, it is essential to reflect on its impact and future potential in relationship therapy.

Positive Impact of CBT:
CBT has proven to be an effective approach for improving communication, resolving conflicts, and strengthening emotional bonds in relationships. Ongoing practice and the development of evidence-based techniques will further enhance its outcomes.

Practical Example:
Continuous studies on CBT's effectiveness in various relationship contexts refine and validate interventions, ensuring they remain relevant and effective.

Transformative Potential:
CBT has the potential to transform how people understand and

manage their relationships. By providing practical and evidence-based tools, CBT empowers individuals to develop healthy and fulfilling relationships.

Practical Example:
Implementing CBT-based prevention programs in schools and communities can educate individuals early about healthy relationship skills, fostering a more connected and empathetic society.

Future Visions:
The future of CBT in relationships involves the continued integration of new research, technologies, and therapeutic approaches. Collaboration among researchers, clinicians, and educators will be key to advancing CBT practice.

Practical Example:
Establishing partnerships between universities, mental health clinics, and community organizations to conduct collaborative research and develop innovative training programs.

Case Study Example
Case: Marcos and Daniela

Couple's Background:
Marcos and Daniela have been married for 12 years and have faced challenges related to communication and stress management. They decided to seek therapy to strengthen their relationship and learn new skills to address their challenges.

Intervention:

Mindfulness Integration:
The therapist introduced mindfulness practices during CBT sessions to help Marcos and Daniela develop greater awareness and acceptance of their thoughts and emotions. They practiced

breathing exercises and meditation together.

Personalized CBT:
The therapist conducted a detailed initial assessment to develop a personalized treatment plan. Interventions were tailored to Marcos and Daniela's specific needs and characteristics, including their learning preferences and cultural background.

New Therapeutic Approaches:

Acceptance and Commitment Therapy (ACT) techniques were used to help them accept difficult emotions and commit to actions promoting a meaningful relationship.
Compassion-Focused Therapy (CFT) was introduced to help them develop self-compassion and compassion for each other, enhancing empathy and mutual understanding.
Results:
After several weeks of therapy, Marcos and Daniela reported significant improvements in communication and stress management. Mindfulness practices, along with ACT and CFT techniques, helped them develop a more balanced and compassionate view of themselves and their relationship. They felt more connected and satisfied, resulting in a stronger and more resilient partnership.

Final Thoughts
Being well within oneself is the foundation upon which a relationship therapist builds their work. Much like a sturdy tree with deep, healthy roots, a therapist who nurtures their well-being can weather emotional storms and provide robust support to clients seeking guidance.

Authenticity and empathy—the cornerstones of the therapeutic relationship—stem from internal balance. A therapist who practices self-reflection, self-compassion, and a balanced lifestyle can connect genuinely with clients, listen attentively, and respond wisely.

Without personal stability, therapists risk emotional fatigue and burnout. Regular self-care practices, professional supervision, and time away from work are crucial to maintaining the equilibrium necessary for effective therapy.

Ultimately, a therapist's well-being is both a personal benefit and a professional responsibility. By prioritizing self-care, therapists can provide a stable and transformative space where relationships can flourish, and healing can occur. Remember: to care for others, one must first care for oneself.

ACKNOWLEDGMENTS

Being well within oneself is the foundation upon which a relationship psychotherapist builds their work. Consider a robust tree: its deep, healthy roots allow it to withstand strong winds, provide shade, and nurture those who seek refuge beneath its canopy. Similarly, a psychotherapist who nurtures their own well-being can offer genuine and effective support to their clients.

The authenticity and empathy that are essential to the therapeutic relationship emanate from a place of internal balance. When a therapist is emotionally aligned, they are capable of truly connecting with their clients, listening attentively, and responding wisely. Constant self-reflection, the practice of self-compassion, and the pursuit of a balanced life enable the therapist to remain present without being overwhelmed by their unresolved personal issues.

Imagine trying to save someone from drowning while struggling to keep your own head above water. Without the security of their own equilibrium, a therapist can easily succumb to emotional exhaustion and burnout. For this reason, it is essential that therapists nurture themselves mentally and emotionally through regular self-care, supervision, and moments of disconnection from work.

The well-being of the therapist is not only a personal benefit but also a professional responsibility. Being well within oneself allows the therapist to be a beacon of stability for their clients, guiding them with clarity and confidence through their emotional storms. Ultimately, a balanced therapist can provide a safe and transformative therapeutic space where relationships can be strengthened, and true healing can occur.

Always remember: to care for others, one must first care for oneself. Self-care is an ongoing practice, a commitment to oneself that directly reflects the ability to transform lives and relationships. And that, undoubtedly, is the essence of successful therapeutic work.

ABOUT THE AUTHOR

Michel Lopes

Michel Lopes é um psicólogo licenciado com uma paixão por compreender e melhorar os relacionamentos humanos. Com anos de experiência em terapia individual e de casais, ele se especializou nas áreas de dependência emocional e dinâmicas relacionais. Michel possui formação avançada em Terapia Cognitivo-Comportamental (TCC), Psicoterapia de Casais e Famílias e Terapia Sexual, o que lhe proporciona um conjunto diversificado de habilidades para ajudar seus clientes a lidar com as complexidades de suas vidas emocionais e relacionais.

A abordagem de Michel combina técnicas baseadas em evidências com um profundo senso de empatia e compromisso em promover conexões autênticas. Seu trabalho é inspirado pela crença de que relacionamentos saudáveis — seja consigo mesmo ou com os outros — estão no centro do bem-estar e da realização pessoal.

Além de sua prática clínica, Michel é um escritor e educador dedicado, compartilhando seus insights por meio de workshops, mídias sociais e publicações. Seu foco em traduzir conceitos psicológicos complexos em ferramentas práticas e acessíveis faz com que seu trabalho ressoe com um público amplo.

A trajetória de Michel como psicoterapeuta é profundamente pessoal. Sua dedicação em ajudar os outros vem de sua curiosidade ao longo da vida sobre o comportamento humano e sua própria jornada de autoconhecimento e crescimento pessoal. Ele acredita que todo indivíduo possui o potencial de criar relacionamentos significativos e satisfatórios, e sua missão é guiá-los nesse caminho.

Quando não está trabalhando, Michel gosta de explorar seu lado criativo como DJ e produtor audiovisual, paixões que lhe permitem conectar-se com as pessoas de maneiras diferentes e dinâmicas. Essa mistura de percepção artística e psicológica alimenta sua abordagem inovadora à terapia e ao desenvolvimento pessoal.

Michel Lopes continua a inspirar e capacitar indivíduos a cultivarem relacionamentos mais saudáveis e satisfatórios, acreditando firmemente que a transformação começa de dentro para fora. Seu trabalho é um testemunho do poder da compreensão, da conexão e da coragem de crescer.